D0776823

The
Quotable
FARMER

MBI

First published in 2005 by MBI, an imprint of MBI Publishing Company, Galtier Plaza, Suite 200, 380 Jackson Street, St. Paul, MN 55101-3885 USA

MBI titles are also available at discounts in bulk quantity for industrial or sales-promotional use. For details write to Special Sales Manager at MBI Publishing Company, Galtier Plaza, Suite 200, 380 Jackson Street, St. Paul, MN 55101-3885 USA.

All photographs by Joel Sheagren except pages 20, 86, which are by Lee Klancher; and pages 76, 90, 93, which are by Randy Leffingwell.

ISBN-13: 978-0-7603-2268-0
ISBN-10: 0-7603-2268-6

Editor: Amy Glaser
Designer: Mandy Iverson

Printed in China

Animals are such agreeable friends,

they *ask no questions*, they *pass no criticisms*.

George Eliot

What a man *is*

depends on his character;

but what he *does,*

and what *we think of what he does,*

depends on his circumstances.

⁓

George Bernard Shaw

Farming looks **mighty** *easy*

when your plow is a pencil

and you're *a thousand miles*

from the corn field.

—｜—

Dwight D. Eisenhower

Determine *never* to be idle.

No person will have occasion to complain

of the want of time who never loses any.

It is wonderful *how much may be done if we are always doing*.

⊷⊱⊶

Thomas Jefferson

Cut your own wood,

and it will warm you twice.

⊶⊷

Anonymous

He who has *patience* may accomplish anything.

—‡—

Rabelais

Life is *what we make it*,

always has been,

always will be.

—✦—

Grandma Moses

The man who *believes* he can do it,

is probably right,

and so is the man who believes he can't.

＊Ⅰ＊

Anonymous

Each blade of *grass*

has its spot on earth

whence *it draws its life*,

its *strength*;

and so is man

rooted to the land

from which he

draws his faith

together with his life.

Joseph Conrad

Gardens, scholars say, are the first sign of

commitment to a community.

When people plant corn they are saying,

let's stay here.

And by their *connection* to the land,

they are *connected* to one another.

—†—

Anne Raver

A plant is like a self-willed man,

out of whom we can obtain *all* which we desire,

if we will only treat him *his own way*.

⋅⊹⋅

Goethe

I like to see a man *proud* of the place in which he lives.

I like to see a man live so that his place *will be proud of him*.

Abraham Lincoln

There is something basic

about protecting land

by taking it off the market.

People should be able to enjoy

where they live

while at the same time

protect the plants and animals

around them.

—

Tom Hanks

There is as much dignity

in *tilling a field*

as in *writing a poem.*

Booker T. Washington

Every man has a lurking wish

to appear *considerable*

in his native place.

·:·

Samuel Johnson

If a man has *good* corn, or wood, or boards, or pigs to sell,

or can make *better* chairs or knives, crucibles, or church organs,

than anybody else, you will find a broad, hard-beaten road

to his house, tho it be in the woods.

❖

Ralph Waldo Emerson

A man's stature is *measured*

by what *he does with what he has.*

❈

Anonymous

God gives all men

all earth to love.

But, *since man's heart is small,*

ordains for each one spot

shall prove *beloved over all.*

—⊹—

Rudyard Kipling

Experience is not

what happens to a man;

it is what a man *does*

with what happens to him.

᠁

Aldous Huxley

Farmers are *the salt of the earth.*

✥

Anonymous

Early to bed, early to rise

makes a man *healthy*, *wealthy*, and *wise*.

—†—

Anonymous

You know you're

an old-tractor nut . . .

if you've *never* lied

to your spouse . . .

except a little *about tractors.*

Roger Welsch

Work is a *necessity* for man.

Man invented the *alarm clock*.

Pablo Picasso

Many men owe

the grandeur of their lives to

their tremendous *difficulties*.

Charles G. Spurgeon

Every man's *work* is a portrait of himself.

━┼━

Anonymous

It is thus with farming;

If you do *one* thing late, you will be *late* in all your work.

—┼—

Cato the Elder

If you would like

to *leave footprints*

in the sands of time,

you had better

wear work shoes.

Herbert V. Prochnow

Always take your work

more seriously

than you take yourself.

❖

Anonymous

Happiness depends on ourselves.

—✦—

Aristotle

We all have hometown appetites.

Every other person is a bundle of longing

for the simplicities of good taste

once enjoyed on the farm or in the hometown

he or she left behind.

—⁂—

Clementine Paddleford

A man *thinks as well* through his legs and arms as *his brain*.

Henry David Thoreau

One man's sunset is another

man's *sunrise*.

⊷⊹⊶

Anonymous

No one knows

what he can do *'til he tries*.

✥

Publilius Syrus

Look at those cows

and remember that

the *greatest scientists*

in the world

have never discovered

how to make grass into milk.

Michael Pupin

I have nothing to offer

but *blood*, *toil*, *tears*, and *sweat*.

Winston Churchill

The farmer is the *only man* in our economy

who buys everything he buys at retail,

sells everything he sells at wholesale,

and pays the freight both ways.

John F. Kennedy

I was once at a tractor show watching a proud gent carefully roll his fully and beautifully restored Allis WC off the truck bed to take it to the exhibit area.

He took a *handkerchief* from his pocket and gently *flicked some road dust from the manifold.*

I turned to his wife and said,

"I'll bet he doesn't treat you like that."

Somewhat wistfully she replied, *"He used to."*

—†—

Roger Welsch

It makes all the difference

whether the shepherd loves the *fleece* or the *flock*.

⋅╂⋅

Anonymous

All the world's a stage,

and every father plays a *supporting role*.

⊷‡⊶

Anonymous

It is not necessary that

a man should earn his living

by the sweat of his brow,

unless he sweats easier

than I do.

Henry David Thoreau

You know you're an old-tractor nut . . .

if your wife catches you *glassy-eyed*,

fantasizing and *breathing hard*

. . . about a tractor.

—✦—

Roger Welsch

Nobody ever *drowned*

in his own sweat.

⁜

Ann Landers

The rung of a ladder was never meant to *rest* upon,

but to *enable* a man to put his other foot higher.

⊷┼⊶

Thomas H. Huxley

Farming is not really

a *business*;

it is an occupation.

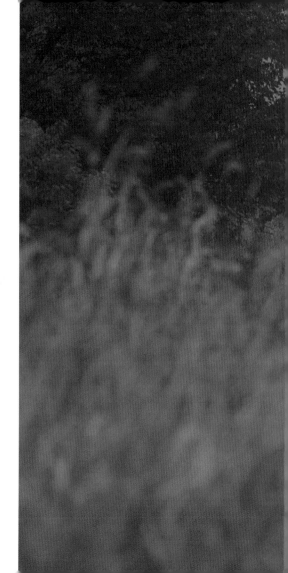

William E. Woodward

The first farmer was

the *first man*,

and all historic nobility

rests on possession

and use of *land*.

—⊢—

Ralph Waldo Emerson

ABOUT THE PHOTOGRAPHERS

Joel Sheagren has been shooting commercially in advertising for 25 years. His photography draws on the pulse of the human spirit, using a sense of place, environment, and natural lighting to bring an epic nature to his work. He lives with his wife and business partner Kim, their two children, and three sled dogs in Minneapolis, Minnesota.

Lee Klancher has been publishing photographs for more than 15 years, in everything from *Minnesota Monthly* magazine to *ATV Rider*. His latest book, *The Tractor in the Pasture*, features landscape photography of abandoned tractors.

Randy Leffingwell has more than 30 books in print and is known for his fantastic photography. Leffingwell discovered photography as an architectual engineer student at Kansas Universtiy and hasn't looked back. He lives in Santa Barbara, California, with his wife, Carolyn.